CONTENTS

Introduction

Guess the player from the career path? Completed it, mate.

Now we're taking on manager career paths!

Split into three sections based on their difficulty, this book will take you from the lows of football league management to world cup winning managers. We'll travel across the world, and from the 1800s to present day to bring you the journeys of 125 professional football managers.

We'll give you teams that the person has taken control of in a managerial role – this could be caretaker, interim, or in the early days – secretary, but it will be in chronological order. Questions will include youth teams for clubs and nations as it could point to interesting origins that could help you guess correctly.

You can work your way through this book in any fashion, but we suggest that you play with friends, with the first person to guess the answer correctly winning that question.

Thank you for buying this book, we really appreciate it and hope you'll have a great time solving the questions!

2) KICK-OFF CLASSICS

1) Who has managed Benfica (2000), Uniao de Leiria (2001 - 2002), Porto (2002 - 2004), Chelsea (2004 - 2007), Inter Milan (2008 - 2010), Real Madrid (2010 - 2013), Chelsea (2013 - 2015), Manchester United (2016 - 2018), Tottenham Hotspur (2019 - 2021), Roma 2021 - 2024), and Fenerbahce (2024 - present, as of December 2024)?

2) Who has managed Reggiana (1995 - 1996), Parma (1996 - 1998), Juventus (1999 – 2001), AC Milan (2001 - 2009), Chelsea (2009 - 2011), Paris Saint-Germain (2011 - 2013), Real Madrid (2013 - 2015), Bayern Munich (2016 - 2017), Napoli (2018 - 2019), Everton (2019 - 2021), and Real Madrid (2021 - present, as of December 2024)?

3) Who has managed East Stirlingshire (1974), St Mirren (1974 - 1978), Aberdeen (1978 - 1986), Scotland (1985 - 1986), and Manchester United (1986 - 2013)?

4) Who has managed Barcelona B (2007 - 2008), Barcelona (2008 - 2012), Bayern Munich (2013 - 2016), and Manchester City (2016 - present, as of December 2024)?

5) Who has managed Vancouver Royal Canadians (1967),

Fulham (1968), Ipswich Town (1969 - 1982), England (1982 - 1990), PSV Eindhoven (1990 - 1992), Sporting CP (1992 - 1994), Porto (1994 - 1996), Barcelona (1996 - 1997), PSV Eindhoven (1998 - 1999), and Newcastle United (1999 - 2004)?

6) Who has managed Newcastle United (1992 - 1997), Fulham (1997 - 1999), England (1999 - 2000), Manchester City (2001 - 2005), and Newcastle United (2008)?

7) Who has managed Liverpool (1985 - 1991), Blackburn Rovers (1991 - 1995), Newcastle United (1997 - 1998), Celtic (Caretaker 2000), and Liverpool (2011 - 2012)?

8) Who has managed Limerick (Player-manager 1991 - 1992), Preston North End (1992), Blackpool (1994 - 1996), Notts County (1997 - 1999), Bolton Wanderers (1999 - 2007), Newcastle United (2007 - 2008), Blackburn Rovers (2008 - 2010), West Ham United (2011 - 2015), Sunderland (2015 - 2016), England (2016), Crystal Palace (2016 - 2017), Everton (2017 - 2018), West Bromwich Albion (2020 - 2021), and Leeds United (2023)?

9) Who has managed AC Milan Primavera (1982 - 1986), AC Milan (Caretaker 1987), AC Milan (1991 - 1996), Real Madrid (1996 - 1997), AC Milan (1997 - 1998), Roma (1999 - 2004), Juventus (2004 - 2006), Real Madrid (2006 - 2007), England (2007 - 2012), Russia (2012 - 2015), and Jiangsu Suning (2017 - 2018)?

10) Who has managed Fiorentina (2001 - 2002), Lazio (2002 - 2004), Inter Milan (2004 - 2008), Manchester City (2009 - 2013), Galatasaray (2013 - 2014), Inter Milan (2014 - 2016), Zenit Saint Petersburg (2017 - 2018), Italy (2018 - 2023), and Saudi Arabia (2023 - 2024)?

11) Who has managed Barcelona B (2008 - 2011), Roma (2011 - 2012), Celta (2013 - 2014), Barcelona (2014 - 2017), Spain (2018 - 2022), and Paris Saint-Germain (2023 - present, as of December 2024)?

12) Who has managed Mainz 05 (2001 - 2008), Borussia Dortmund (2008 - 2015), and Liverpool (2015 - 2024)?

13) Who has managed Arezzo (2006), Arezzo (2007), Bari (2007 - 2009), Atalanta (2009 - 2010), Siena (2010 - 2011), Juventus (2011 - 2014), Italy (2014 - 2016), Chelsea (2016 - 2018), Inter Milan (2019 - 2021), Tottenham Hotspur (2021 - 2023), and Napoli (2023 - present, as of December 2024)?

14) Who has managed Hartlepool United (1965 - 1967), Derby County (1967 - 1973), Brighton & Hove Albion (1973 - 1974), Leeds United (1974), and Nottingham Forest (1975 - 1993)?

15) Who has managed South Melbourne (1996 - 2000),

Australia U17 (2000 - 2005), Australia U20 (2005 - 2007), Panachaiki (2008), Whittlesea Zebras (2009), Brisbane Roar (2009 - 2012), Melbourne Victory (2012 - 2013), Australia (2013 - 2017), Yokohama F. Marinos (2018 - 2021), Celtic (2021 - 2023), and Tottenham Hotspur (2023 - present, as of December 2024)?

16) Who has managed Universidad de Chile (1988 - 1989), Palestino (1990 - 1991), O'Higgins (1992 - 1993), Unversidad Catolica (1994 - 1996), Palestino (1998), Liga de Quito (1999 - 2000), San Lorenzo (2001 - 2002), River Plate (2002 - 2003), Villarreal (2004 - 2009), Real Madrid (2009 - 2010), Malaga (2010 - 2013), Manchester City (2013 - 2016), Hebei China Fortune (2016 - 2018), West Ham United (2018 - 2019), and Real Betis (2020)?

17) Who has managed Real Madrid B (2014 - 2016), Real Madrid (2016 - 2018), and Real Madrid (2019 - 2021)?

18) Who has managed Racing Club (2006), Estudiantes (2006 - 2007), River Plate (2007 - 2008), San Lorenzo (2009 - 2010), Catania (2011), Racing Club (2011), and Atletico Madrid (2011 - present, as of December 2024)?

19) Who has managed Carlisle United (1949 - 1951), Grimsby Town (1951 - 1954), Workington (1954 - 1955), Huddersfield Town (1956 - 1969), and Liverpool (1959 - 1974)?

20) Who has managed Ipswich Town (1955 - 1963), England (1963 - 1974), and Birmingham City (1977 - 1978)?

21) Who has managed Victoria Bammental (1996 - 2000), TSG Hoffenheim (2000 - 2005), Bayern Munich (2019 - 2021), Germany (2021 - 2023), and Barcelona (2024 - present, as of December 2024)?

22) Who has managed Dunfermline Athletic (1960 - 1964), Hibernian (1964 - 1965), Scotland (1965), Celtic (1965 - 1978), and Leeds United (1978), Scotland (1978 - 1985)?

23) Who has managed Halmstad (1976 - 1980), Bristol City (1982), Oddevold (1982), Orebro (1983 - 1984), Malmo (1985 - 1989), Neuchatal Xamax (1990 - 1992), Switzerland (1992 - 1995), Inter Milan (1995 - 1997), Blackburn Rovers (1997 - 1998), Inter Milan (Caretaker 1999), Grasshoppers (1999 - 2000), FC Copenhagen (2000 - 2001), Udinese (2001), United Arab Emirates (2002 - 2004), Viking (2004 - 2005), Finland (2006 - 2007), Fulham (2007 - 2010), Liverpool (2010 - 2011), West Bromwich Albion (2011 - 2012), England (2012 - 2016), Crystal Palace (2017 - 2021), Watford (2022), and Crystal Palace (2023 - 2024)?

24) Who has managed Le Touquet (1973 - 1976), Noeux-les-Mines (1976 - 1982), Lens (1982 - 1985), Paris Saint-Germain (1985 - 1988), France (1992 - 1993), France U18

(1994 - 1996), France U20 (1996 - 1997), Liverpool (1998 - 2004), Lyon (2005 - 2007), and Aston Villa (2010 - 2011)?

25) Who has managed Vigor Lamezia (1986 - 1987), Puteolana (1987 - 1988), Cagliari (1988 - 1991), Napoli (1991 - 1993), Fiorentina (1993 - 1997), Valencia (1997 - 1999), Atletico Madrid (1999 - 2000), Chelsea (2000 - 2004), Valencia (2004 - 2005), Parma (2007), Juventus (2007 - 2009), Roma (2009 - 2011), Roma (2009 - 2011), Inter Milan (2011 - 2012), Monaco (2012 - 2014), Greece (2014), Leicester City (2015 - 2017), Nantes (2017 - 2018), Fulham (2018 - 2019), Roma (2019), Sampdoria (2019 - 2021), Watford (2021 - 2022), Cagliari (2023 - 2024), and Roma (2024 - present, as of December 2024)?

26) Who has managed Newell's Old Boys II (1987 - 1990), Newell's Old Boys (1990 - 1992), Atlas (1993 - 1995), America (1995 - 1996), Velez Sarsfield (1997 - 1009), Espanyol (1998), Argentina (1998 - 2004), Argentina U23 (2004), Chile (2007 - 2011), Athletic Bilbao (2011 - 2013), Marseille (2014 - 2015), Lazio (2016), Lille (2017), Leeds United (2017 - 2022), Uruguay (2023 - present, as of December 2024), and Uruguay U23 (2023 - 2024)?

27) Who has managed FC Frauenfeld (1994 - 1995), VfB Stuttgart (Caretaker 1996), VfB Stuttgart (1996 - 1998), Karlsruher SC (1999 - 2000), Adanaspor (2000 - 2001), Tirol Innsbruck (2001 - 2002), Austria Wien (2003 - 2004), and Germany (2006 - 2021)?

28) Who has managed Ajax Youth (1988 - 1990), Ajax (1991 - 1997), Barcelona (1997 - 2000), Netherlands (2000 - 20001), Netherlands U20 (2001), Barcelona (2002 - 2003), AZ (2005 - 2009), Bayern Munich (2009 - 2011), Netherlands (2012 - 2014), Manchester United (2014 - 2016), and Netherlands (2021 - 2022)?

29) Who has managed PSV (1987 - 1990), Fenerbahce (1990 - 1991), Valencia (1991 - 1993), Valencia (1994), Netherlands (1995 - 1998), Real Madrid (1998 - 1999), Real Betis (2000), South Korea (2001 - 2002), PSV (2002 - 2006), Australia (2005 - 2006), Russia (2006 - 2010), Chelsea (Caretaker 2009), Turkey (2010 - 2011), Anzhi Makhachkala (2012 - 2013), Netherlands (2014 - 2015), Chelsea (Caretaker 2015 - 2016), China U21 (2018 - 2019), and Curacao (2020 - 2021)?

30) Who has managed Chelsea (Player Manager 1996 - 1998), Newcastle United (1998 - 1999), Feyenoord (2004 - 2005), LA Galaxy (2007 - 2008), and Terek Grozny (2011)?

31) Who has managed Netherlands (1998 - 2000), Sparta Rotterdam (2001 - 2002), Barcelona (2003 - 2008), Galatasaray (2009 - 2010), and Saudi Arabia (2011 - 2013)?

32) Who has managed Ajax (1985 - 1988), Barcelona

(1988 - 1996), and Catalonia (2009 - 2013)?

33) Who has managed Degerfors IF (1977 - 1978), IFK Goteborg (1979 - 1982), Benfica (1982 - 1984), Roma (1984 - 1987), Fiorentina (1987 - 1989), Benfica (1989 - 1992), Sampdoria (1992 - 1997), Lazio (1997 - 2001), England (2001 - 2006), Manchester City (2007 - 2008), Mexico (2008 - 2009), Ivory Coast (2010), Leicester City (2010 - 2011), Guangzhou R&F (2013 - 2014), Shanghai SIPG (2014 - 2016), Shenzen (2016 - 2017), and Phillipines (2018 - 2019)?

34) Who has managed Nancy (1984 - 1987), Monaco (1987 - 1994), Nagoya Grampus Eight (1995 - 1996), and Arsenal (1996 - 2018)?

35) Who has managed Real Madrid U17 (1986 - 1993), Real Madrid Castilla (1993 - 1995), Valladoli (1995 - 1996), Osasuna (1996), Extremadura (1997 - 1999), Tenerife (2000 - 2001), Valencia (2001 - 2004), Liverpool (2004 - 2010), Inter Milan (2010), Chelsea (Caretaker 2012 - 2013), Napoli (2013 - 2015), Real Madrid (2015 - 2016), Newcastle United (2016 - 2019), Dalian Professional (2019 - 2021), Everton (2021 - 2022), and Celta Vigo (2023 - 2024)?

36) Who has managed Rayo Vallecano (2003), Real Madrid Castilla (2008 - 2009), Spain U19 (2010 - 2013), Spain U20 (2010 - 2014), Spain U21 (2012 - 2014), Porto

(2014 - 2016), Spain (2016 - 2018), Real Madrid (2018), Sevilla (2019 - 2022), Wolverhampton Wanderers (2022 - 2023), and West Ham United (2024 - present, as of December 2024)?

37) Who has managed Monaco (2001 - 2005), Juventus (2006 - 2007), Marseille (2009 - 2012), and France (2012 - present, as of December 2024)?

38) Who has managed CSA (1982), Juventude (1982 - 1983), Brasil de Pelotas (1983), Al-Shabab (1984 - 1985), Pelotas (1986), Juventude (1986 - 1987), Gremio (1987), Goias (1988), Al Qadisiya (1988 - 1990), Kuwait (1990), Coritiba (1990), Criciuma (1991), Al-Ahli (1991), Al Qadisiyia (1992), Gremio (1993 - 1996), Jubilo Iwata (1997), Palmeiras (1998 - 2000), Cruzeiro (2000 - 2001), Brazil (2001 - 2002), Portugal (2003 - 2004), Chelsea (2008 - 2009), Buyodkor (2009 - 2010), Palmeiras (2010 - 2012), Brazil (2012 - 2014), Gremio (2014 - 2015), Guangzhou Evergrande (2015 - 2017), Palmeiras (2018 - 2019), Cruzeiro (2020 - 2021), Gremio (2021), Athletico Paranaense (2022), and Atletico Mineiro (2023 - 2024)?

39) Who managed Liverpool (1974 - 1983)?

40) Who has managed AC Milan Youth (1972 - 1974), AC Milan (1974), AC Milan (1974 - 1976), Juventus (1976 - 1986), Inter Milan (1986 - 1991), Juventus (1991 - 1994), Bayern Munich (1994 - 1995), Cagliari (1995 - 1996),

Bayern Munich (1996 - 1998), Fiorentina (1998 - 2000), Italy (2000 - 2004), Benfica (2004 - 2005), VfB Stuttgart (2005 - 2006), Red Bull Salzburg (2006 -2008), Republic of Ireland (2008 - 2013), and Vatican City (2010)?

41) Who has managed Real Madrid Castila (1987 - 1990), Real Madrid (1994), Real Madrid (Caretaker 1996), Real Madrid (1999 - 2003), Spain (Besiktas 2004 - 2005), and Spain (2008 - 2016)?

42) Who has managed Sampdoria Youth (1982 - 1985), Pontedera (1985 - 1986), Siena (1986 - 1987), Pistoiese (1987 - 1988), Carrarese (1988 - 1989), Cesena (1989 - 1991), Lucchese (1991 - 1992), Atalanta (1992 - 1993), Napoli (1993 - 1994), Juventus (1994 - 1999), Inter Milan (1999 - 2000), Juventus (2001 - 2004), Italy (2004 - 2006), Italy (2008 - 2010), Guangzhou Evergrande (2012 - 2014), and China (2016 - 2019)?

43) Who has managed Manchester United (1945 - 1969), Great Britain (1948), Scotland (1958), and Manchester United (1970 - 1971)?

44) Who has managed Asser Boys (1953 - 1954), JOS (1960 - 1964), AFC (1964 - 1965), Ajax (1965 - 1971), Barcelona (1971 - 1974), Netherlands (1974), Ajax (1975 - 1976), Barcelona (1976 - 1978), Los Angeles Aztecs (1979 - 1980), 1. FC Koln (1980 - 1983), Netherlands (1984 - 1985), Netherlands (1986 - 1988), Bayern Leverkusen

(1988 - 1989), and Netherlands (1990 - 1992)?

45) Who has managed Chelsea Reserves (2006 - 2008), Watford (2008 - 2009), Reading (2009), Swansea City (2010 - 2012), Liverpool (2012 - 2015), Celtic (2016 - 2019), Leicester City (2019 - 2023), and Celtic (2023 - present, as of December 2024)?

46) Who has managed Espanyol (2009 - 2012), Southampton (2013 - 2014), Tottenham Hotspur (2014 - 2019), Paris Saint-Germain (2021 - 2022), Chelsea (2023 - 2024), and United States (2024 -present, as of December 2024)?

47) Who has managed FC Augsburg II (2007 - 2008), Mainz 05 (2009 - 2014), Borussia Dortmund (2015 - 2017), Paris Saint-Germain (2018 -2020), Chelsea (2021 - 2022), and Bayern Munich (2023 - 2024)?

48) Who has managed Watford (2011 - 2012), Burnley (2012 - 2022), and Everton (2023 - present, as of December 2024)?

49) Who has managed Lorca Deportiva (2004 - 2006), Almeria (2006 - 2008), Valencia (2008 - 2012), Spartak Moscow (2012), Sevilla (2013 - 2016), Paris Saint-Germain (2016 - 2018), Arsenal (2018 - 2019), Villarreal (2020 - 2022), and Aston Villa (2022 - present, as of December 2024)?

50) Who has managed Arsenal (2019 - present, as of December 2024)?

2) MIDFIELD CHALLENGES

1) Who has managed Blackburn Rovers (1979 - 1981), Everton (1981 - 1987), Athletic Bilbao (1987 - 1989), Manchester City (1989 - 1990), Everton (1990 - 1993), Xanthi (1994), Notts County (1995), Sheffield United (1995 - 1997), Everton (1997 - 1998), and Ethnikos Piraeus (1998 - 1999)?

2) Who has managed Palermo Youth (1974 - 1983), Licata (1983 - 1986), Foggia (1986 - 1987), Parma (1987), Messina (1988 - 1989), Foggia (1989 - 1994), Lazio (1994 - 1997), Roma (1997 - 1999), Fenerbahce (1999 - 2000), Napoli (2000), Salernitana (2001 - 2002), Avellino (2003 - 2004), Lecce (2004 - 2005), Brescia (2006), Lecce (2006), Red Star Belgrade (2008), Foggia (2010 - 2011), Pescara (2011 - 2012), Roma (2012 - 2013), Cagliari (2014), Lugano (2015 - 2016), Pescara (2017 - 2018), Foggia (2021 - 2022), and Pescara (2023 - 2024)?

3) Who has managed Hakoah Wien (1933 - 1935), Enschede (1935 - 1937), Hakoah Wien (1937 - 1938), Ujpest (1938 - 1939), Vasas (1945), Ciocanul Bucuresti (1946), Ujpest (1947), Kispest (1947 - 1948), Padova (1949 - 1950), Triestina (1950 - 1951), Quilmes (1953), APOEL (1953), AC Milan (1953 - 1955), Vicenza (1955 - 1956), Honved (1956 - 1957), Sao Paulo (1957 - 1958), Porto (1958 - 1959), Benfica (1959 - 1962), Penarol (1962), Austria (1964), Benfica (1965 - 1966), Servette (1966 - 1967), Panathinaikos (1967), Austria Wien (1973),

and Porto (1973)?

4) Who has managed FV Rockenhausen (1972), 1. FC Saarbrucken (1972 - 1973), Kickers Offenbach (1974 - 1975), Werder Bremen (1976), Borussia Dortmund (1976 - 1978), Arminia Bielefeld (1978 - 1979), Fortuna Dusseldorf (1979 - 1980), Werder Bremen (1981 - 1995), Bayern Munich (1995 - 1996), 1. FC Kaiserslautern (1996 - 2000), Greece (2001 - 2010), and Hertha BSC (2012)?

5) Who has managed Leeds United (1961 - 1974), England (1974 - 1977), United Arab Emirates (1977 - 1980), Al-Nasr (1980 - 1984), and Al-Ahly (1984)?

6) Who has managed Fusignano (1973 - 1976), Alfonsine (1976 - 1977), Bellaria (1977 - 1978), Cesena Youth (1978 - 1982), Rimini (1982 - 1983), Fiorentina Youth (1983 - 1984), Rimini (1984 - 1985), Parma (1985 - 1987), AC Milan (1987 - 1991), Italy (1991 - 1996), AC Milan (1996 - 1997), and Atletico Madrid (1998 - 1999)?

7) Who has managed Motherwell (1994 - 1998), Hibernian (1998 - 2001), Rangers (2001 - 2006), Scotland (2007), Scotland B (2007), Birmingham City (2007 - 2011), Aston Villa (2011 - 2012), Nottingham Forest (2012 - 2013), Genk (2014 - 2015), Zamalek (2016), and Scotland (2018 - 2019)?

8) Who has managed AFC Bournemouth (2008 - 2011), Burnley (2011 - 2012), AFC Bournemouth (2012 - 2020),

and Newcastle United (2021 - present, as of December 2024)?

9) Who has managed Coventry City (1996 - 2001), Southampton (2001 - 2004), Celtic (2005 - 2009), Middlesbrough (2009 - 2010), and Scotland (2013 - 2017)?

10) Who has managed Grantham Town (1987 - 1989), Shepshed Charterhouse (1989), Wycombe Wanderers (1990 - 1995), Norwich City (1995), Leicester City (1995 - 2000), Celtic (2000 - 2005), Aston Villa (2006 - 2010), Sunderland (2011 - 2013), Republic of Ireland (2013 - 2018), and Nottingham Forest (2019)?

11) Who has managed Leeds United (1998 - 2002), Aston Villa (2003 - 2006), and Al-Ahli (2010 - 2011)?

12) Who has managed Crystal Palace (1976 - 1980), Queens Park Rangers (1980 - 1984), Barcelona (1984 - 1987), Tottenham Hotspur (1987 - 1991), England (1994 - 1996), Australia (1996 - 1998), Crystal Palace (1998 - 1999), Middlesbrough (Joint manager 2000 - 2001), and Leeds United (2002 - 2003)?

13) Who has managed Lincoln City (1972 - 1977), Watford (1977 - 1987), Aston Villa (1987 - 1990), England (1990 - 1993), Wolverhampton Wanderers (1994 - 1995), Watford (1996), Watford (1997 - 2001), and Aston Villa (2002 - 2003)?

14) Who has managed Rangers (1986 - 1991), Liverpool (1991 - 1994), Galatasaray (1995 - 1996), Southampton (1996 - 1997), Torino (1997), Benfica (1997 - 1999), and Blackburn Rovers (2000 - 2004)?

15) Who has managed Juventus Youth (1994 - 2003), Crotone (2003 - 2004), Crotone (2005 - 2006), Genoa (2006 - 2010), Inter Milan (2011), Palermo (2011 - 2013), Genoa (2013 - 2016), and Atalanta (2016 - present, as of December 2024)?

16) Who has managed Bristol Rovers (1996 - 2001), Queens Park Rangers (2001 - 2006), Plymouth Argyle (2006 - 2007), Leicester City (2007 - 2008), Blackpool (2009 - 2012), Crystal Palace (2012 - 2013), Millwall (2014 - 2015), Queens Park Rangers (2016 - 2018), Grimsby Town (2019 - 2020), and Swindon Town (2024 - present, as of December 2024)?

17) Who has managed Germany (2004 - 2006), Bayern Munich (2008 - 2009), United States (2011 - 2016), Hertha BSC (2019 - 2020), and South Korea (2023 - 2024)?

18) Who has managed AFC Bournemouth (1983 - 1992), West Ham United (1994 - 2001), Portsmouth (2002 - 2004), Southampton (2004 - 2005), Portsmouth (2005 - 2008), Tottenham Hotspur (2008 - 2012), Queens Park Rangers (2012 - 2015), Jordan (2016), and Birmingham City (2017)?

19) Who has managed Derby County (2018 - 2019), Chelsea (2019 - 2021), Everton (2022 - 2023), Chelsea (Caretaker 2023), and Coventry City (2024)?

20) Who has managed Millwall (1982 - 1986), Arsenal (1986 - 1995), Leeds United (1996 - 1998), and Tottenham Hotspur (1998 - 2001)?

21) Who has managed Blackburn Rovers (2010 - 2012), DPMM FC (2013 - 2017), Brunei (2014), Melbourne Victory (2021), and Torpedo Kutaisi (2023 - present, as of December 2024)?

22) Who has managed Tottenham Hotspur (Caretaker 1997), Tottenham Hotspur (Caretaker 1998), Newcastle United (Caretaker 2008), Newcastle United (2009 - 2010), Birmingham City (2011 - 2012), Norwich City (2012 - 2014), Brighton & Hove Albion (2014 - 2019), Nottingham Forest (2020 - 2021), and Ghana (2023 - 2024)?

23) Who has managed Hapoel Petah Tikva Youth (1972 - 1986), Hapoel Petah Tikva (1986 - 1991), Maccabi Tel Aviv (1991 - 1995), Hapoel Haifa (1995 - 1996), Maccabi Tel Aviv (1996 - 2000), Maccabi Haifa (2000 - 2002), Israel (2002 - 2006), Chelsea (2007 - 2008), Portsmouth (2009 - 2010), West Ham United (2010 - 2011), Partizan Belgrade (2012), Ghana (2014 - 2017), and Zambia (2022 - present, as of December 2024)?

24) Who has managed Stia (1990 - 1991), Faellese (1991 - 1993), Cavriglia (1993 - 1996), Antella (1996 - 1998), Valdema (1998 - 1999), Sansovino (2000 - 2003), Sangiovannese (2003 - 2005), Pescara (2005 - 2006), Arezzo (2006 - 2007), Avellino (2007), Verona (2007 - 2008), Perugia (2008 - 2009), Grosseto (2010), Alessandria (2010 - 2011), Sorrento (2011 - 2012), Empoli (2012 - 2015), Napoli (2015 - 2018), Chelsea (2018 - 2019), Juventus (2019 - 2020), and Lazio (2021 - 2024)?

25) Who has managed New York City FC (2016 - 2018), Nice (2018 - 2020), Crystal Palace (2021 - 2023), Strasbourg (2023 - 2024), and Genoa (2024 - present, as of December 2024)?

26) Who has managed Swansea City (2007 - 2009), Wigan Athetic (2009 - 2013), Everton (2013 - 2016), Belgium (2016 - 2022), Portugal (2023 - present, as of December 2024)?

27) Who has managed Fulham (2003 - 2007), Real Sociedad (2007 - 2008), Coventry City (2008 - 2010), Athlitiki Enosi Larissa (2011 - 2012), Wales (2012 - 2017), Sunderland (2017 - 2018), Hebei China Fortune (2018 - 2019), Atromitos (2022 - 2023), AEL Limassol (2024), and OH Leuven (2024 - present, as of December 2024)?

28) Who has managed Middlesbrough (2001 - 2006), England (2006 - 2007), Twente (2008 - 2010), VfL Wolfsburg (2010 - 2011), Nottingham Forest (2011), Twente (2012 - 2013), Derby County (2013 - 2015),

Newcastle United (2015 - 2016), Derby County (2016 - 2017), Queens Park Rangers (2018 - 2019), and Jamaica (2024 - present, as of December 2024)?

29) Who has managed Livingston (2005 - 2006), Wycombe Wanderers (2006 - 2008), Colchester United (2008 - 2009), Norwich City (2009 - 2012), Aston Villa (2012 - 2015), Blackburn Rovers (2015 - 2016), Wolverhampton Wanderers (2016 - 2017), Stoke City (2018), and Ipswich Town (2018 - 2021)?

30) Who has managed Queens Park Rangers (1988 - 1989), Sheffield Wednesday (1991 - 1995), Birmingham City (1996 - 2001), and Crystal Palace (2001 - 2003)?

31) Who has managed Monaco (1999 - 2001), Lille (2002 - 2008), Lyon (2008 - 2011), Nice (2012 - 2016), Southampton (2016 - 2017), Leicester City (2017 - 2019), and Saint-Etienne (2019 - 2021)?

32) Who has managed Vitesse (2000 - 2001), Ajax (2001 - 2005), Benfica (2005 - 2006), PSV (2006 - 2007), Valencia (2007 - 2008), AZ (2009), Feyenoord (2011 - 2014), Southampton (2014 - 2016), Everton (2016 - 2017), Netherlands (2018 - 2020), Barcelona (2020 - 2021), and Netherlands (2023 - present, as of December 2024)?

33) Who has managed Netherlands Women (1987), HFC Haarlem (1987 - 1989), SVV (1989 - 1991), Dordrecht (1991 - 1992), Netherlands (1992 - 1994), PSV (1994 -

1998), Rangers (1998 - 2001), Netherlands (2002 - 2004), Borussia Monchengladbach (2004 - 2005), United Arab Emirates (2005), South Korea (2005 - 2006), Zenit Saint Petersburg (2006 - 2009), Belgium (2009 - 2010), AZ (2009 - 2010), Russia (2010 - 2012), PSV (2012 - 2013), AZ (2013 - 2014), Serbia (2014), Sunderland (2015), Fenerbahce (2016 - 2017), Netherlands (2017), Sparta Rotterdam (2017 - 2018), Utrecht (2018 - 2019), Feyenoord (2019 - 2021), Iraq (2021), ADO Den Haag (2022 - 2023), and Curacao (2024 - present, as of December 2024)?

34) Who has managed Swindon Town (1989 - 1991), Newcastle United (1991 - 1992), West Bromwich Albion (1992 - 1993), Tottenham Hotspur (1993 - 1994), Guadalajara (1995), Shimizu S-Pulse (1996 - 1998), Dinamo Zagreb (1999), Yokohama F. Marinos (2000 - 2001), Al-Ittihad (2001), Racing Club (2002 - 2003), Tokyo Verdy (2003 - 2005), Beitar Jerusalem (2006), Huracan (2007), and Cerro Porteno (2008)?

35) Who has managed Lisieux (1983 - 1985), Toulouse (1985 - 1989), Lille (1989 - 1992), Saint-Etienne (1992 - 1994), Sochaux (1994 - 1995), Lyon (2000 - 2002), France (2002 - 2004), Tottenham Hotspur (2004), and Auxerre (2005 - 2006)?

36) Who has managed Acireale (2001 - 2002), Pisoiese (2002 - 2003), Livorno (2003 - 2004), Reggina (2004 - 2007), Sampdoria (2007 - 2009), Napoli (2009 - 2013), Inter Milan (2013 - 2014), Watford (2016 - 2017), Torino (2018 - 2020), Cagliari (2021 - 2022), and Napoli (2023 -

2024).

37) Who has managed Ipswich Town (Caretaker 2002), Hibernian (2004 - 2006), West Bromwich Albion (2006 - 2009), Celtic (2009 - 2010), Middlesbrough (2010 - 2013), Coventry City (2015 - 2016), Blackburn Rovers (2017 - 2022), Sunderland (2022 - 2023), and Birmingham City (2024)?

38) Who has managed Hajduk Split (2001 - 2002), Croatia U21 (2004 - 2006), Croatia (2006 - 2012), Lokomotiv Moscow (2012 - 2013), Besiktas (2013 - 2015), West Ham United (2015 - 2017), Al-Ittihad (2018 - 2019), West Bromwich Albion (2019 - 2020), Beijing Guoan (2021 - 2022), Watford (2022 - 2023), and Al-Fateh (2023 - 2024)?

39) Who has managed Bradford City (1998 - 2000), Sheffield Wednesday (2000 - 2001), Wigan Athletic (2001 - 2007), Derby County (2007 - 2008), and Ipswich Town (2011 - 2012)?

40) Who has managed Charlton Athletic (1991 - 2006), and West Ham United (2006 - 2008)?

41) Who has managed AFC Bournemouth (1992 - 1994), Gillingham (1995 - 1999), Bristol City (1999 - 2000), Portsmouth (2000), Stoke City (2002 - 2005), Plymouth Argyle (2005 - 2006), Stoke City (2006 - 2013), Crystal Palace (2013 - 2014), West Bromwich Albion (2015 - 2017), Middlesbrough (2017 - 2019), and Sheffield

Wednesday (2020)?

42) Who managed Tottenham Hotspur (1958 - 1974)?

43) Who has managed Coslada (1999 - 2000), Merida (2000), Murcia (2000 - 2001), Tenerife (2001 - 2002), Getafe (2003), Alaves (2003 - 2004), Poli Ejido (2004 - 2005), Rayo Vallecano (2006 - 2010), Real Betis (2010 - 2013), West Bromwich Albion (2014), Real Betis (2014 - 2016), Deportivo La Coruna (2017), Las Palmas (2019 - 2022), Malaga (2022 - 2023), OFI Crete (2023 - 2024), Almeria (2024), and Tenerife (2024 - present, as of December 2024)?

44) Who has managed Elche Youth (1989 - 1990), Elche B (1990 - 1992), Alcoyano (1992 - 1994), Levante (1994 - 1995), Logrones (1995 - 1996), Barcelona B (1996 - 1997), Lleida (1997 - 1998), Rayo Vallecano (1998 - 2001), Real Betis (2001 - 2002), Espanyol (2002), Malaga (2003 - 2004), Sevilla (2005 - 2007), Tottenham Hotspur (2007 - 2008), Real Madrid (2008 - 2009), CSKA Moscow (2009), Dnipro Dnipropetrovsk (2010 - 2014), and Malaga (2016)?

45) Who has managed Academica (2009 - 2010), Porto (2010 - 2011), Chelsea (2011 - 2012), Tottenham Hotspur (2012 - 2013), Zenit Saint Petersburg (2014 - 2016), Shanghai SIPG (2016 - 2017), and Marseille (2019 - 2021)?

46) Who has managed Brondby (2002 - 2006), Getafe (2007 - 2008), Spartak Moscow (2008 - 2009), Mallorca

(2010 - 2011), Swansea City (2012 - 2014), Lekhwiya (2014 - 2015), and Al-Rayyan (2016 - 2018)?

47) Who has managed Millwall (1992 - 1996), Republic of Ireland (1996 - 2002), Sunderland (2003 - 2006), Wolverhampton Wanderers (2006 - 2012), Ipswich Town (2012 - 2018), Republic of Ireland (2018 - 2021), APOEL (2020 - 2021), Cardiff City (2021), and Blackpool (2023)?

48) Who has managed Sunderland (2006 - 2008), and Ipswich Town (2009 - 2011)?

49) Who has managed Macclesfield Town (2006 - 2007), Milton Keynes Dons (2007 - 2008), Blackburn Rovers (2009 - 2010), Milton Keynes Dons (2009 - 2010), Notts County (2010 - 2011), Blackpool (2013 - 2014), and Reading (2022 - 2023)?

50) Who has managed Borussia Dortmund II (2011 - 2015), Huddersfield Town (2015 - 2019), Schalke 04 (2019 - 2020), Young Boys (2021 - 2022), and Norwich City (2023 - 2024)?

4) FINAL THIRD HEROES

1) Who has managed Lyon (2011 - 2014), Aston Villa (2015 - 2016), and Montreal Impact (2017 - 2019)?

2) Who has managed Hamburger SV (1995 - 1997), 1. FC Nurnberg (1997 - 1998), Werder Bremen (1998 - 1999), Eintracht Frankfurt (1999 - 2001), VfB Stuttgart (2001 - 2004), Bayern Munich (2004 - 2007), VfL Wolfsburg (2007 - 2009), Schalke 04 (2009 - 2011), VfL Wolfsburg (2011 - 2012), Fulham (2014), Shandong Luneng Taishan (2016 - 2017), and Hertha BSC (2022)?

3) Who has managed Ayr United (1991 - 1993), Colchester United (1994), Ipswich Town (1994 - 2002), Derby County (2003 - 2005), Heart of Midlothian (2005), Southampton (2005 - 2008), Scotland (2008 - 2009), Scotland B (2009), Crystal Palace (2010 - 2011), and Apollon Limassol (2012)?

4) Who has managed Wycombe Wanderers (2003 - 2004), Portsmouth (2008 - 2009), Gabala (2010 - 2011), and Granada (2017)?

5) Who has managed Genoa (1912 - 1927), Italy (1913 - 1914), Roma (1927 - 1929), Napoli (1929 - 1935), Athletic Bilbao (1935 - 1937), AC Milan (1937), Genoa (1937 - 1940), and Genoa (1946 - 1948)?

6) Who has managed Villarreal Youth (2004 - 2005),

Pontevedra (2007 - 2008), Cadiz (2008 - 2010), Villarreal B (2010 - 2011), Olympiacos Volos (2011), Kerkyra (2011 - 2012), Almeria (2012 - 2013), Osasuna (2013 - 2014), Malaga (2014 - 2016), Rubin Kazan (2018 - 2019), Watford (2018 - 2019), Valencia (2020 - 2021), Al Sadd (2021 - 2022), and Leeds United (2023)?

7) Who has managed Sion (2013), Palermo (2013), OFI Crete (2014), Pisa (2015 - 2016), Pisa (2016 - 2017), AC Milan Primavera (2017), AC Milan (2017 - 2019), Napoli (2019 - 2021), Valencia (2022 - 2023), Marseille (2023 - 2024), and Hajduk Split (2024 - present, as of December 2024)?

8) Who has managed Atalanta Youth (1990 - 1997), Atalanta (Caretaker 1993 - 194), Lecce (1997 - 1998), Verona (1998 - 2000), Venezia (2000 - 2001), Parma (2002 - 2004), Roma (2004), Fiorentina (2005 - 2010), Italy (2010 - 2014), Galatasaray (2014), Valencia (2016), Al-Nasr (2017 - 2018), Genoa (2018 - 2019), and Fiorentina (2020 - 2021)?

9) Who has managed Fortuna Koln (1997 - 1998), 1. FC Koln (1998 - 1999), Xerez (2001 - 2002), Shakhtar Donetsk (2003 - 2004), Levante (2004 - 2005), Getafe (2005 - 2007), Real Madrid (2007 - 2008), Besiktas (2010 - 2011), Malaga (2013 - 2014), and Dalian Yifang (2018 - 2019)?

10) Who has managed Croatia U21 (2012 - 2013), Croatia (2013 - 2015), Eintracht Frankfurt (2016 - 2018), Bayern

Munich (2018 - 2019), Monaco (2020 - 2022), and VfL Wolfsburg (2022 - 2024)?

11) Who has managed Caxias (1991 - 1992), Veranopolis (1992 - 1995), Ypiranga -RS (1996), Caxias (1998), Veranopolis (1998), Caxias (1999 - 2000), Gremio (2001 - 2003), Sao Caetano (2003 - 2004), Corinthians (2004 - 2005), Atletico Mineiro (2005), Palmeiras (2006), Al Ain (2007), Internacional (2008 - 2009), Al Wahda (2010), Corinthians (2010 - 2013), Corinthians (2014 - 2016), Brazil (2016 - 2022), and Flamengo (2023 - 2024)?

12) Who has managed Auxerre (1961 - 2005), and Lens (2007)?

13) Who has managed Italy (1912), Torino (1912 - 1922), Italy (1921), Italy (1924), AC Milan (1924 - 1926), and Italy (1929 - 1948)?

14) Who has managed Estrela Amadora Youth (2005 - 2007), 1o Dezembro, Odivelas (2008 - 2009), Pinhalnovense (2009 - 2011), Aves (2011 - 2012), Pacos Ferreira (2012 - 2013), Porto (2013 - 2014), Pacos Ferreira (2014 - 2015), Braga (2015 - 2016), Shakhtar Donetsk (2016 - 2019), Roma (2019 - 2021), Lille (2022 - 2024), and AC Milan (2024 - present, as of December 2024)?

15) Who has managed Corbeil-Essonnes (1994 - 1998), Saint-Etienne (2001), Dijon (2002 - 2007), Le Mans (2007 - 2008), Lille (2008 - 2013), Roma (2013 - 2016),

Marseille (2016 - 2019), Lyon (2019 - 2021), Al Nassr (2022 - 2023), and Napoli (2023)?

16) Who has managed Brazil (2006 - 2010), Brazil U23 (2008), Internacional (2012 - 2013), and Brazil (2014 - 2016)?

17) Who has managed Bayern Munich (1970 - 1975), Borussia Monchengladbach (1975 - 1979), Borussia Dortmund (1979 - 1981), Barcelona (1981 - 1983), Bayern Munich (1983 - 1987), 1. FC Koln (1991), Schalke 04 (1992 - 1993), and Borussia Dortmund (2000)?

18) Who has managed AC Milan (2009 - 2010), Inter Milan (2010 - 2011), and Antalyaspor (2017)?

19) Who has managed Uruguay (1928 - 1932), Central Espanol (1935), Montevideo Wanderers (1938), Uruguay (1935 - 1941), and Penarol (1945)?

20) Who has managed Torino Youth (1964 - 1967), Prato (1968 - 1969), Italy U23 (1969 - 1965), and Italy (1975 - 1986)?

21) Who has managed Sheffield United (Secretary 1899 - 1932)?

22) Who has managed Northampton Town (1907 - 1912),

Leeds City (1912 - 1918), Huddersfield Town (1921 - 1925), and Arsenal (1925 - 1934)?

23) Who has managed Echallens (1993 - 1995), Yverdon Sport (1997 - 2000), Servette (2000 - 2002), Zurich (2003 - 2007), Hertha BSC (2007 - 2009), Borussia Monchengladbach (2011 - 2015), Nice (2016 - 2018), Borussia Dortmund (2018 - 2020), and Nice (2022 - 2023)?

24) Who has managed Barcelona (1961 - 1963), Espanyol (1963 - 1966), Zurich (1966 - 1967), Toronto Falcons (1968), Cordoba (1968 - 1969), Spain (1969 - 1980), Barcelona (1980), Al-Hilal (1982 - 1986), Murcia (1986), Malaga (1987 - 1988), Elche (1988 - 1989), and Paraguay (1992)?

25) Who has managed Estudiantes (1971), Estudiantes (1973 - 1976), Deportivo Cali (1976 - 1978), San Lorenzo (1979), Colombia (1979 - 1981), Estudiantes (1982 - 1983), Argentina (1983 - 1990), Sevilla (1992 - 1993), Boca Junior (1996), Guatemala (1998), Libya (1999 - 2000), and Estudiantes (2003 - 2004)?

5) ANSWERS

Kick-Off Classics

1) Jose Mourinho
2) Carlo Ancelotti
3) Alex Ferguson
4) Pep Guardiola
5) Bobby Robson
6) Kevin Keagan
7) Kenny Dalglish
8) Sam Allardyce
9) Fabio Capello
10) Roberto Mancini
11) Luis Enrique
12) Jurgen Klopp
13) Antonio Conte
14) Brian Clough
15) Ange Postecoglou
16) Manuel Pellegrini
17) Zinedine Zidane
18) Diego Simeone
19) Bill Shankly
20) Alf Ramsay
21) Hansi Flick
22) Jock Stein
23) Roy Hodgson
24) Gerrard Houllier
25) Claudio Ranieri
26) Marcelo Bielsa
27) Joachim Low

28) Louis van Gaal
29) Guus Hiddink
30) Ruud Gullit
31) Frank Rijkard
32) Johan Cruyff
33) Sven Goran Erikson
34) Arsene Wenger
35) Rafael Benitez
36) Julen Loptegui
37) Didier Deschamps
38) Luis Felipe Scolari
39) Bob Paisley
40) Giovanni Trapattoni
41) Vicente del Bosque
42) Marcelo Lippi
43) Matt Busby
44) Rinus Michels
45) Brendan Rodgers
46) Mauricio Pochettino
47) Thomas Tuchel
48) Sean Dyche
49) Unai Emery
50) Mikel Arteta

Midfield Challenges

1) Howard Kendall
2) Zdenek Zeman
3) Bela Guttman
4) Otto Rehhagel
5) Don Revie
6) Arrigo Sacchi
7) Alex McLeish
8) Eddie Howe
9) Gordon Strachan
10) Martin O'Neill
11) David O'Leary
12) Terry Venables
13) Graham Taylor
14) Graeme Souness
15) Gian Piero Gasperini
16) Ian Holloway
17) Jurgen Klinsmann
18) Harry Redknapp
19) Frank Lampard
20) George Graham
21) Steve Kean
22) Chris Hughton
23) Avram Grant
24) Maurizio Sarri
25) Patrick Viera
26) Roberto Martinez
27) Chris Coleman
28) Steve McClaren
29) Paul Lambert
30) Trevor Francis
31) Claude Puel
32) Ronald Koeman

33) Dick Advocaat
34) Ossie Ardiles
35) Jacques Santini
36) Walter Mazzari
37) Tony Mowbray
38) Slaven Bilic
39) Paul Jewell
40) Alan Curbishley
41) Tony Pulis
42) Bill Nicholson
43) Pepe Mel
44) Juande Ramos
45) Andre Villas-Boas
46) Michael Laudrup
47) Mick McCarthy
48) Roy Keane
49) Paul Ince
50) David Wagner

Final Third Heroes

1) Remi Garde
2) Felix Magath
3) George Burley
4) Tony Adams
5) William Garbutt
6) Javi Gracia
7) Gennaro Gattuso
8) Cesare Prandelli
9) Bernd Schuster
10) Niko Kovac
11) Tite
12) Guy Roux
13) Vittorio Pozzo
14) Paulo Fonseca
15) Rudi Garcia
16) Dunga
17) Udo Lattek
18) Leonardo
19) Alberto Suppici
20) Enzo Beardot
21) John Nicholson
22) Herbert Chapman
23) Lucien Favre
24) Laszlo Kubala
25) Carlos Bilardo